THE LONDON
·RLH·
Remembered

RLH 63 working the last few days on route 230.

Front cover:

Preserved RLHs 23 and 32 leave Staines Bridge for their home bases having attended the 'Showbus' rally at Thorpe Park on 7 September 1980.

Half title page:

Preserved RLH 32 outside the Greater Manchester Museum of Transport.

Title page: (opposite)

The last RLHs 23 and 29 to visit Dalston Garage, which closed shortly afterwards, are shown during the Anniversary Tour, ready to depart on 19 April 1981. The person walking between the two RLHs is Bernie Brown, a former mechanical charge-hand at Dalston Garage and who was connected with negotiations regarding the preservation of the first RLH, RLH 23 which was obtained from this garage.

THE LONDON
°RLH°
Remembered

PETER
GASCOINE

 Roadmaster Publishing

ACKNOWLEDGEMENTS

The assistance of David Pring and Maurice Bateman for various research, plus the PSV Circle for certain of the details recorded in the disposals section is gratefully acknowledged by the author.

Also gratefully acknowledged are the undermentioned for use of their photographs:

Maurice Bateman 36 top & lower, 37 lower
Paul A. Bateson 38 lower, 58 lower
David Bosher 23 lower
Brian Gentle 57 lower
Brian Goulding 47 lower, 54 top & lower
Malcolm John back cover
London Bus Preservation Group 77
London Country 70
London Transport 39 top & lower, 40
Robert F. Mack 28 top, 32 top
Marco Ghidorzi, London Bus 60, 61 & 62 top & lower, 65

J. C. Parkin 27 top & lower
David Pring 3, 19 top, 24 lower, 48, 58 top
R. Proctor 71 top
P. J. Relf 30 lower, 31 lower, 47 top, 50 top, 69
Trevor Ryall 50 lower
J. G. S. Smith 25 top, 29 lower
A. J. Stoute Front cover, 68 top
Ken Wade 21 top, 38 top
David Waymann 68 lower

The remaining photographs are from the Author's collection, several of which were taken by unidentified photographers and therefore thanks are also passed to these persons.

First published in 1995 in Great Britain by
Roadmaster Publishing
PO Box 176
Chatham
Kent ME5 9AQ

ISBN 1 871814 21 9

British Library Cataloguing in Publication Data
A catalogue record for this book is available from
the British Library

Printed and bound in Great Britain by
Bookcraft (Bath) Ltd, Midsomer Norton, Avon

CONTENTS

An unidentified RLH, working Route 127, turning across the A3 on 16 November 1955.

INTRODUCTION

This publication has been written as a sequel to 'The London RLH' which was produced in 1976. That booklet described the complete history of the RLH whilst in service with both London Transport and London Country between 1950 and 1971. This history is now brought up to date giving such details as disposals and those thought to be in current preservation ownership.

As the RLH is now over forty years old hopefully through preservation and businesses, we will be able to see on the roads an occasional glimpse of what were London's last lowbridge buses.

Peter Gascoine
Wigan, Lancashire
September 1994

RLH 35 leaving Weybridge for Walton just prior to being withdrawn in 1970.

VEHICLE DETAILS

RLH 1-20
Classified 1RLH1
Registration Numbers   KYY 501-KYY 520
Chassis Type   AEC Regent III model 9612E
Bodywork   Weymann L27/26R (26ft × 7ft 6in)
Height 13ft 4in unladen
Delivery Dates   RLH 1-5 5/50
RLH 6-17 6/50
RLH 18-20 7/50
London Transport Body Nos   7099-7118

RLH 21-76
Classified 2RLH1/1
Registration Numbers   MXX 221-MXX 276
Chassis Type   AEC Regent III model 9613E
Bodywork   Weymann L27/26R (26ft × 7ft 6in)
Height 13ft 4in unladen
Delivery Dates   RLH 21-48 10/52
RLH 49-64 11/52
RLH 65-76 12/52
London Transport Body Nos   8032-8087

RLH 1 poses for the camera shortly after entering service in May 1950 from Amersham Garage.

The RLH vehicles were the only double deck buses of the period fitted with outward opening cab doors as opposed to the normal sliding cab doors.

Country area 'Clippie' complete with Gibson ticket machine.

RLH 13 at Guildford Bus Station. Route 408A was worked by both RLH and RT vehicles throughout the 1960s. On several short routes the destination blinds showed both terminals as seen on RLH 13.

RLH 47 at Walton Odeon with a husband and wife crew in winter uniform.

RLH 14 at the Ottershaw terminus. Front destinations are changed by the conductor from the upper deck on these vehicles, as shown in this view.

RLH 15 at the White Lodge terminus near Chertsey on route 461A, with a crew in summer uniform.

HISTORY OF THE RLH 1950-1971
WHILST IN PASSENGER SERVICE WITH LONDON TRANSPORT & LONDON COUNTRY

Following the need to replace the ageing and mixed lowbridge fleet of vehicles in 1950 London Transport was given the opportunity to obtain twenty AEC Regent IIIs with lowbridge bodies, built to a standard pattern by Weymann's of Addlestone and originally intended for the Midland General Company. This batch of vehicles were purchased and formed the 'RLH' (Regent Low Height) class.

The vehicles were completed and all delivered to London Transport in Country area green livery; the first six entering service from Amersham garage in May and June 1950 on route 336 with the remainder of the batch being allocated to Addlestone and Godstone and entering service by July 1950.

Having found the RLH a most suitable lowbridge vehicle, especially as the chassis was very similar to the large number of standard RT vehicles then entering service a repeat order for a further 56 RLHs was placed. These vehicles were all delivered between October and December 1952; the first thirty-two being green for the country area followed by the remaining twenty-four being red for the central area. The central area vehicles were all allocated to Harrow Weald (14) and Merton (10) with the Country area vehicles being dispersed to Godstone (8), Guildford (8), Addlestone (7), East Grinstead (4) and Amersham (5). This second batch of vehicles was very similar to the first batch but noticeable by some minor variances, the most obvious being their polished aluminium radiators. Other differences were chrome hand rails and the used ticket box on the back platform. London Transport vehicles normally gave excellent destination information and it was therefore curious to see the RLHs were devoid of rear destination boxes. However for a time route number stencils were carried on the exterior of the lower back window, whilst advertisments were later carried on the normal back 'between decks' panel. Advertising on RLH vehicles was slightly different to other London Transport buses both on the interior and exterior. London vehicles have always found advertising on the front panels between decks very popular but the RLH was never to be seen wearing such advertising, although earlier lowbridge vehicles had; nor were interior adverts possible on the upper deck apart from on the front roof dome of the vehicle, this being due to the single skin roof, bare lights and 'Caution Low Roof' signs fitted to the RLH. The interior of the lowbridge RLH was very different to the highbridge vehicles especially on the upper deck, where the sunken offside gangway and rows of bench type seats were always causing a problem for the conductor with a full bus. Passengers on the lower deck offside were also often found to leave the vehicle with a bruised head after forgetting to 'lower their head' when leaving their seat.

By 1953 the London Transport lowbridge fleet had reached its peak with a total of seventy-six vehicles, being operated on a larger number of routes than ever before. Coronation Day 2 June 1953 saw RLH 45 working on Green Line service 708 between East Grinstead and London, Victoria. 1954 saw RLH 44 being allocated to Reigate to operate the heavily used weekday short workings on route 447. 16 February 1955 saw two Country area green vehicles being transferred to the Central Area for use on routes 248/9. Vehicles involved were RLH 22 and 23 which were eventually painted red for the purpose. From May 1955 Staines garage occasionally borrowed RLHs from Addlestone at weekends to work duplicate journeys on Green Line route 725.

RLH 1 was transferred to the central area in November 1956 followed by RLH 9 in October 1957 both repainted into red livery.

The strike in the summer of 1958 saw the beginning of the decline for the RLH. Central route 127 was withdrawn and various other amendments were made to both Central and Country area routes reducing the overall Monday-Friday schedule requirement from 67 to 53 (16 Central and 37 Country). A new route (178) operated out of Dalston from 13 May 1959. RLH's 7, 29, 49 and 52 were repainted red to make up the 14 vehicle allocation for the May commencement. Further minor changes took place during the next few years the 410 losing RLH's early in November 1964 and in 1965 route 336 was converted to RF operation with the 461A being converted to RT operation. This resulted in only 16 RLHs being required for scheduled work in the Country Area on Monday-Friday.

June 1965 saw the only livery change which involved all Central area vehicles receiving flake grey relief bands in place of the cream used previously upon repaint. Country area vehicles were not affected.

The decline in the Country area continued with route 447 losing its RLH allocation after 24 December 1967 leaving only Addlestone and Guildford garages operating the RLH. The next drastic reduction was in the Central area when route 230 was converted to MBS operation on 14 June 1969.

With the formation of London Country Bus Services on 1 January 1970, 17 Country area RLHs were transferred to this operator – these being: RLH 13, 14, 21, 24, 25, 26, 31, 32, 33, 34, 35, 36, 44, 45, 46, 47 and 50. Legal lettering was changed to read Bell Street, Reigate, Surrey and the fleet name panels were painted out together sadly with the triangle badge on the radiator. London Country fleet names were applied gradually but no other livery change took place. In the spring of 1970 London Country announced the RLHs would be withdrawn and replaced by new one-man operated single deck vehicles (SMs). The date for the withdrawal was given as 31 July 1970 and being the last day of the month all the vehicles were to be de-licenced by midnight therefore meaning that late evening journeys would probably be performed by RFs. RLH 35 was allocated a late duty and worked into Addlestone garage at 2309 off route 436 just before a surprise RLH 44 arrived in the garage at 2317 having worked some late journeys on route 461A between Ottershaw and Walton, the crew having demanded their allocated RLH for the second half of their duty!! RLH 44 then remained at Addlestone pending its conversion into a mobile uniform stores for London Country. All other RLHs were ferried to Garston (now Watford) garage for storage.

The remaining London Transport central area RLHs were then set for withdrawal; routes 248/A being converted to SMS operation from 18 September 1970. This left just one route, the 178 which was the last central area route to commence RLH operation on 13 May 1959 and now the last to operate them. The date was announced as 16 April 1971 and RLH 61 duly emerged as D3 for the evening peak service on that day. Unlike the Country area route 178 operated the full service for the day with RLHs and on the last journey of all from Stratford to Clapton Pond at 2035, RLH 61 was fully laden for this ceremonial journey. Leaving Clapton Pond on time RLH 61 entered Dalston garage a few minutes late at 2117 after which is was reprieved for a further day when on the 17

April it operated a private hire covering former RLH territory both in the Country and Central area. It was then stored at Poplar for a few days before being exported to Canada.

The RLH was now only a memory to the travelling public of the London suburbs, but with a large number of the vehicles being re-sold for further use their story up to the year 1971 is far from complete . . .

Ottershaw terminus sees RLH 11 on a cold winter's morning, 20 February 1965.

DATES OF OVERHAULS

When vehicles were overhauled they retained their original bodies. Dates given are dates ex-works.

RLH					RLH				
1	2/53,	11/56,	1/62		39	5/56,	4/60		
2	2/53,	12/56,	4/61		40	6/56,	7/60		
3	3/53,	1/57,	3/62		41	6/56,	9/60		
4	4/53,	1/57,	7/62		42	7/56,	10/60		
5	5/53,	1/57,	7/62		43	7/56,	9/60		
6	7/53,	2/57,	5/62		44	3/56,	1/60,	9/64	
7	6/53,	2/57,	8/62		45	3/56,	8/59,	6/64	
8	3/53,	1/57,	4/62		46	11/55,	3/59,	3/64	
9	8/53,	9/57,	12/62		47	12/55,	6/59,	5/64	
10	3/54,	10/57,	9/62		48	5/56,	6/60		
11	3/54,	12/57,	3/63		49	1/56,	2/60,	11/64	
12	5/54,	3/58,	2/63		50	1/56,	7/59,	6/64	
13	6/54,	7/58,	6/63		51	6/56,	8/60		
14	8/54,	7/58,	8/63		52	7/56,	10/60,	1/65	
15	4/53,	1/57,	11/61		53	2/56,	10/59,	8/64	
16	3/54,	10/57,	10/62		54	2/56,	12/59,	10/64	
17	4/54,	3/58,	4/63		55	3/56,	2/60,	11/64	
18	5/54,	4/58,	4/63		56	4/56,	3/60,	12/64	
19	6/54,	6/58,	10/62		57	3/56,	4/60,	12/64	
20	7/54,	7/58,	7/63		58	1/56,	9/59,	8/64	
21	8/55,	9/58,	8/63		59	8/56,	3/61,	6/65	
22	9/55,	5/59,	4/64		60	8/56,	12/60,	3/65	
23	11/55,	2/59,	2/64		61	8/56,	6/61,	10/65	
24	8/55,	9/58,	10/63		62	9/56,	5/61,	8/65	
25	8/55,	8/58,	9/63		63	9/56,	6/61,	10/65	
26	10/55,	1/59,	1/64		64	9/56,	7/61,	11/65	
27	9/55,	10/58,	11/63		65	2/56,	11/59,	10/64	
28	10/55,	11/58,	12/63		66	9/56,	4/61,	7/65	
29	12/55,	4/59,	4/64		67	10/56,	8/61,	12/65	
30	8/55,	9/58,	10/63		68	10/56,	9/61,	1/66	
31	10/55,	12/58,	12/63		69	10/56,	11/60,	2/65	
32	8/55,	10/58,	11/63		70	11/56,	1/61,	4/65	
33	2/56,	9/59,	7/64		71	10/56,	8/61,	12/65	
34	11/55,	1/59,	2/64		72	10/56,	10/61,	1/66	
35	11/55,	4/59,	4/64		73	11/56,	1/61,	3/65	
36	3/56,	12/59,	9/64		74	11/56,	3/61,	5/65	
37	4/56,	5/69			75	12/56,	10/61		
38	5/56,	6/60			76	12/56,	5/62		

LIVERY

RLH 1-52 delivered in Green Livery.

RLH 53-76 delivered in Red Livery.

RLH	1	Repainted Red 11/56	Ex Green Livery.
RLH	7	Repainted Red 4/59	Ex Green Livery.
RLH	9	Repainted Red 9/57	Ex Green Livery.
RLH	22	Repainted Red 9/55	Ex Green Livery.
RLH	23	Repainted Red 11/55	Ex Green Livery.
RLH	29	Repainted Red 4/59	Ex Green Livery.
RLH	49	Repainted Red 4/59	Ex Green Livery.
RLH	52	Repainted Red 4/59	Ex Green Livery.

From June, 1965, all Red repaints received flake grey bands in place of cream.

VEHICLE TRANSFERS TO LONDON COUNTRY 1 JANUARY 1970

On the formation of London Country Bus Services Ltd., the 17 green country area vehicles were transferred to this operator from 1 January 1970. The vehicles involved were:

RLH 13, 14, 21, 24, 25, 26, 31, 32, 33, 34, 35, 36, 44, 45, 46, 47, 50.

All allocated to either Addlestone or Guildford garages.

Addlestone Garage showing RLH 21 with RLH 13 and 24 in the background shortly after having been received into London Country ownership.

COUNTRY AREA PICTUREVIEW

RLH 34 at Addlestone Station. This view shows the single skin roof with outside ribbing, but without the roof ventilators carried by the first batch.

This front view of RLH 10 at Addlestone (Dukes Head) clearly shows the small opening vent fitted below the windscreen on the first batch of vehicles only.

RLH 33 travels along the tree-lined Woodham Lane after losing its London Transport fleetnames early in 1970.

RLH 3 at Amersham Garage on 25 April 1962.

RLH 43 shortly after entering service from East Grinstead Garage on Route 428 (East Grinstead-Dormansland). A surprising allocation, as there was no Low Bridge on this route.

Rear view of RLH 50 as it passes through the picturesque village of Send Marsh on its journey to Ripley in August 1965. Note the by now disused route stencil holder.

The rear view of RLH 19 at Addlestone showing the position of the trafficators later fitted to the first batch of vehicles in similar fashion to those on Routemasters.

Built in 1952 this Country Area bus RLH 32, mainly worked from Addlestone and Guildford Garages until withdrawn from service in July 1970. This view shows the bus at the former West Byfleet Station terminus of Route 420.

RLH 47 at Chertsey waits to commence a works journey to Weybridge BAC. Following accident damage the rear offside wing was replaced by beading strip leaving a rather odd effect as can be seen in this view.

RLH 31 at Send in August 1965.

RLH 26 at Addlestone Garage displays 'London Country' fleetnames and legal ownership in July 1970.

RLH 21 passes through Sheerwater Estate on 18 July 1970.

RLH 35 passes through the wash in Amersham Garage.

RLH 36 leaves Weybridge for the British Aircraft Corporation Works on the last day of RLH Country Area operation, 31 July 1970.

RLH 17 working Route 410 on the 4 August 1962 clearly shows off the chrome radiator surround and roof ventilators as fitted to the first batch of vehicles RLH 1-RLH 20.

RLH 33 working route 336 passes through Chesham. Soon after the 336 conversion to RF operation in 1965, RLH 33 was transferred to Guildford where it displaced RLH 11 from the first batch of vehicles.

It's 31 July 1970 and RLH 47 retires from service. Seen here leaving Addlestone Garage it heads for storage at Gaston before its long journey to Hawaii!

On 31 July 1970 all RLHs are withdrawn from passenger service in the London Country fleet. This view shows RLHs 45, 14, 32, 36 and 21 at Addlestone Garage waiting to be ferried to Garston Garage.

Following arrival at Addlestone Garage RLH 31 is stripped of destination blinds, whilst the conductor chats to the garage hands and possibly says, "There will never be another bus quite like the RLH." (Perhaps you know exactly what he meant!)

RLH 35 on this last journey on Route 436 from Woking to Addlestone. At 22.41 with enthusiasts aboard we depart Woking, Commercial Road on this final run to Addlestone.

Woking Station, RLH 35 with Driver Todman about to commence the final run to Addlestone Garage.

CENTRAL AREA PICTUREVIEW

RLH 1 repainted into Central Area red livery seen working Route 248.

RLH 59 at Upminster Station on a very hot summer day. Excellent ventilation is given to both upper deck passengers and the driver with large opening front windows.

Many bridges on Outer London roads had 13ft 9in headroom and RLH 68 just passes under one of these along Route 248.

Another limited headroom bridge was situated in Headstone Drive on Route 230 and RLH 70 squeezes through with very little room to spare!

RLH 57 and RLH 65, in original condition, with front number plates fitted below the radiator, radiator blinds, garage code running plates and devoid of trafficators.

RLH 64 shows the modifications applied in later years which include the fitting of trafficators, rear wheel discs and the painting red of all the sliding window surrounds. Also shown in this view is the revised position of the front number plate and painted garage code.

RLH 71, in original condition, working Route 127 to Raynes Park Station, shortly before the route's withdrawal.

RLH 70 on a very hot autumn day, 2 September 1961, at Kenton (British Rail) Station.

RLH 73 working Route 127 from Merton Garage.

RLH 74 looking smart, having just returned from overhaul complete with 'Lazy Blinds' at Rayners Lane.

RLH 53 nears the end of its life with London Transport when photographed working on Route 178.

RLHs at Clapton Pond terminus.

Alterations to local bus services

STARTING APRIL 17

Bus 178 is having to be altered for two reasons; the present low-height double-deck buses are obsolete and need to be replaced; the route is uneconomic and will have to be converted to one-man-operation if it is to continue. Unfortunately the only buses which London Transport has which are able to pass under the low railway bridges in Carpenters Road are single-deckers which are too long and too wide to negotiate some of the roads served by the present bus 178. The route will have, therefore, to be withdrawn in its present form

The London RLH was finally withdrawn in 1971 when Route 178 was also withdrawn. The above cutting is taken from publicity information produced by London Transport.

RLH 55 at Upminster Station in July 1964.

RLH 48 at Addlestone Garage in January 1962.

THE UNUSUAL VIEW

Timber suppliers Gliksten of Stratford in East London operated former RLH 1 as a staff bus, painted in a deep cream livery. Seen here at their premises on 27 February 1965. This unusual view of RLH 51 shows it waiting to pick up Office Cleaning Services personnel outside the Queens Building at London's Heathrow Airport during 1967. Its LT green livery has been modified by painting the upper deck panels white.

RLH 32 passes Maidstone & District DL 45 in Addlestone. Both vehicles are lowbridge; bodywork by Weymann's, whose factory is just ½ mile from the above view. The Atlantean had failed and awaits mechanical attention on possibly its first road test in the late summer of 1959.

RLH 17 was just one of many green RLHs to work from Harrow Weald (HD) on central area route 230, often covering for red RLHs away being overhauled etc. It is seen here in Headstone Drive, Wealdstone on 18 April 1965.

Preserved RLH 32 leaves Addlestone Garage with a group of enthusiasts to commemorate 10 years of the demise of the Country RLH in July 1980.

Former RLH 61 in the yard of Travelways, Kingston, Ontario, Canada on 22 April 1978.

INTERIOR VIEWS

A view of both saloons with the layout accommodating the sunken gangway clearly visible and the 'Caution Low Roof' signs. Upstairs can be seen the four across seating.

This interior view shows how much space was available for advertisers inside the bus.

GARAGE ALLOCATIONS

RLH 1	5/50-9/56MA	11/56-8/58HD	8/58-5/59HD(+)	5/59-11/61D	2/62-12/64RD
RLH 2	8/50-7/55MA 11/64-12/64WY(+)	7/55-11/56GD 1/65-2 65DS(+)	12/56-9/60WY	9/60-10/60D	10/60-11/64WY
RLH 3	5/50-7/55MA 10/60-9/61RD	7/55-12/55GF 9/61-12/61WY	12/55MA 3/62-11/64MA	12/55-3/56HD 11/64-2/65MA(+)	3/56-10/60MA
RLH 4	5/50-7/55MA 5/56-6/56MA	7/55-12/55WY 6/56-11/56HD	12/55-2/56HD 1/57-4/62MA	2/56-3/56MA 7/62-11/64GD	3/56-5/56HD 11/64-12/64RG(+)
RLH 5	5/50-3/54MA 6/55-12/56WY 2/65-4/66DS(+)	3/54-4/54WY 2/57-5/62GF 4/66-8/66GY(+)	4/54-6/54MA 7/62-8/62RG(+) 8/66-2/67GR(+)	6/54-9/54WY 8/62GF	9/54-6/55MA 8/62-2/65WY
RLH 6	6/50-2/54MA 2/55-9/55WY 11/64-1/65RG(+)	2/54-4/54GD 9/55-6/56MA	4/54-5/54WY 6/56-12/56AL	5/54-8/54GF 2/57-6/62MA	8/54-2/55MA 6/62-11/64GD
RLH 7	6/50-12/56WY 7/66-1/67L(+)	12/56-3/57GD 1/67-10/67PR(+)	3/57-4/59GF	4/59-4/66D	4/66-7/66D(+)
RLH 8	6/50-11/64WY	11/64-1/65WY(+)	1/65DS(+)		
RLH 9	6/50-7/57WY 6/63-12/63CT(+)	10/57-8/58RD 12/63-3/66RD	8/58-5/59RD(+) 3/66-7/66RD(+)	5/59-9/62D	12/62-6/63D(+)
RLH 10	6/50-1/57WY 10/59-11/59D 1/66-2/66WY(+)	1/57-8/57RD 11/59-1/60GD	11/57-5/59WY 1/60-3/60RD	5/59-7/59RG 3/60-6/62GD	7/59-10/59GD 9/62-1/66WY
RLH 11	6/50-5/61WY 11/61-12/61GF	5/61-7/61HD 12/61-11/62WY	7/61-8/61WY 11/62-3/63WR(+)	8/61-10/61WR 3/63-1/66GF	10/61-11/61GD 1/66-5/66GF(+)
RLH 12	6/50-6/65WY	6/65-2/66WY(+)			
RLH 13	6/50-2/54WY 7/58-2/59WY	2/54-6/57MA 2/59-6/70GF	6/57-7/57AL 6/70-8/70RG(+)	7/57-1/58WY 8/70-2/71GR(+)	1/58-3/58GD
RLH 14	6/50-7/70WY	8/70-2/71GR(+)			
RLH 15	6/50-11/56GD 11/64-3/65MA(+)	1/57-9/61WY	12/61-1/62GD	1/62-4/62WY	4/62-11/64MA
RLH 16	7/50-7/62GD	10/62-1/66WY	1/66-2/66WY(+)		
RLH 17	7/50-10/62GD 4/63-11/64GD 2/66-3/66GR(+)	10/62RG 11/64RG(+) 3/66-11/66HD	11/62-12/62GF 12/64-7/65HD 11/66-9/67GR(+)	12/62-2/63WY 7/65-8/65RG(+)	2/63RG 8/65-2/66HD
RLH 18	7/50-10/62GD 2/65-4/66DS(+)	10/62RG 4/66-8/66GY(+)	11/62-12/62RD 8/66-9/67GR(+)	12/62MA	12/62-2/65WY
RLH 19	7/50-10/57GD 4/63-5/63GD	10/57-2/58RG(+) 5/63-11/63RG	6/58-8/62WY 11/63-11/64GD	11/62-3/63RG(+) 11/64-9/65RG(+)	3/63-4/63RG 9/65-10/66GR(+)
RLH 20	7/50-4/63GD	7/63-2/65WY	2/65-4/66DS(+)	4/66-8/66GY(+)	8/66-5/68GR(+)
RLH 21	10/52-2/55GD	2/55-6/55RD	8/55-7/70WY	8/70-2/71GR(+)	
RLH 22	10/52-2/55GD 6/66-11/67D(+)	2/55RG	2/55-4/59RD	5/59-8/59HD(+)	8/59-6/66D
RLH 23	10/52-2/55WY 2/64-6/66D	2/55-9/55RD 6/66-9/67D(+)	11/55-1/59HD	2/59-4/59HD(+)	4/59-12/63RD
RLH 24	10/52-10/63WY	11/63-7/70GF	8/70-2/71GR(+)		
RLH 25	10/52-6/55WY 9/63-7/70WY	8/55-9/57GF 8/70-1/71GR(+)	9/57-10/57RD	10/57-4/58RE(+)	8/58-7/63GF
RLH 26	10/52-12/63WY	1/64-7/70GF	8/70-2/71GR(+)		

RLH 27	10/52-9/63WY 7/68-6/69HD	11/63-2/64RG 6/69-9/69SE(+)	2/64-4/64GD	4/64-2/68RG	2/68-7/68GR(+)
RLH 28	10/52-9/55WY 12/58-11/64GD	11/55-12/55MA 11/64-10/65MA	12/55-4/56HD 10/65-3/66GR(+)	4/56-8/58GD 3/66-11/66HD	8/58-10/58RG(+) 11/66-9/67GR(+)
RLH 29	10/52-10/52GF	10/52-3/59WY	4/59-4/71D	4/71-7/72PR(+)	
RLH 30	10/52WY 10/65-10/67GR(+)	10/52-6/55GF	8/55-7/63WY	10/63-11/64GD	11/64-10/65MA
RLH 31	10/52-11/63GF	1/64-7/70WY	8/70-1/71GR(+)		
RLH 32	10/52-10/57GF	10/57-3/58WY	3/58-5/58GD	5/58-7/70WY	8/70-2/71GR(+)
RLH 33	10/52-8/55GF 10/65-1/66GR(+)	8/55-12/55RD 1/66-7/70GF	2/56-10/57EG 8/70-1/71GR(+)	10/57-5/64GD	8/64-10/65MA
RLH 34	10/52-9/55GF 12/58HD	11/55-8/57MA 2/59-11/63GD	8/57-12/57GD 11/63RG	12/57-2/58RG(+) 2/64-7/70GF	2/58-12/58GD 8/70-1/71GR(+)
RLH 35	10/52-3/64GF 8/70-12/70GR(+)	4/64-11/64GD	11/64-10/65MA	10/65-1/66GR(+)	1/66-7/70WY
RLH 36	10/52-11/64GD	11/64-10/65MA	10/65-1/66GR(+)	1/66-7/70WY	8/70-71GR(+)
RLH 37	10/52-3/63GD 9/65GR(+)	4/63GD(+)	5/63RG	5/63-11/64GD	11/64-9/65RG(+)
RLH 38	10/52-4/60GD	6/60-6/64MA	6/64-8/64WY	8/64-1/65WY(+)	1/65-9/65DS(+)
RLH 39	10/52-10/64GD	10/64-1/65GD(+)			
RLH 40	10/52-11/64GD	11/64-8/65RG(+)			
RLH 41	10/52-5/56GD 1/64-4/64MA	7/56-12/56HD 4/64-6/64MA(+)	12/56-6/60WY 6/64-5/65GR(+)	9/60-5/62RG	5/62-1/64GF
RLH 42	11/52-1/54EG 7/56-11/56HD	1/54-4/54WY 11/56-11/64MA	4/54-5/54GD 11/64-3/65MA(+)	5/54-2/55EG	2/55-5/56GD
RLH 43	10/52-2/55EG 12/60GD	2/55-5/56GD 12/60-3/61HD	7/56-11/56GD 3/61-10/64WY	11/56-8/60GD 10/64-1/65WY(+)	9/60-12/60HD 1/65-9/65GY(+)
RLH 44	10/52-2/54EG 3/56-4/56MA 9/70RG(+) for conversion to 581J	2/54-5/54WY 4/56-5/56WY	5/54-6/54GD 5/56-7/64MA	6/54-7/54EG 10-64-7/70WY	7/54-1/56RG 8/70-9/70WY(+)
RLH 45	10/52-2/54EG 8/70-1/71GR(+)	2/54AL	2/54-2/56EG	3/56-11/64GD	11/64-7/70WY
RLH 46	10/52-5/56MA	5/56-1/64WY	1/64-3/64WY(+)	4/64-7/70GF	8/70-1/71GR(+)
RLH 47	10/52-3/58MA 11/64-7/70WY	3/58-4/58GD 8/70-1/71GR(+)	4/58-11/58WY	11/58-5/64GF	5/64-11/64GD
RLH 48	10/52-2/54MA 7/59-9/59GD 6/60-12/64WY	2/54-10/55WY 9/59-12/59D 1/65-3/65GY(+)	10/55-3/56RD 12/59-2/60MA 3/65-9/65SV(+)	5/56-6/56GD 2/60-3/60D	6/56-7/59GF 3/60-5/60GD
RLH 49	11/52-5/55MA	6/55-11/55AL	1/56-4/59GD	4/59-4/71D	4/71-5/72PR(+)
RLH 50	11/52-11/55MA 2/64GF 12/64-7/70WY	1/56-5/59RG 2/64-3/64WY 8/70-1/71GR(+)	7/59-4/60RG 3/64-4/64GD	4/60-1/64GD 4/64-6/64WY(+)	1/64RG(+) 6/64-12/64RG(+)
RLH 51	11/52-10/55GF	10/55-4/56WY	6/56-6/60MA	8/60-11/64MA	11/64-3/65MA(+)
RLH 52	11/52-5/56GF 5/62-5/63RG 1/65-9/70RD	7/56-11/56HD 5/63-2/64RG(+) 9/70-2/71PR(+)	11/56-4/59GF 2/64-4/64RG 2/71-4/71BK(+)	4/59-9/60D 4/64-9/64RG(+)	11/60-5/62HD 9/64-11/64D
RLH 53	11/52-8/58HD 10/71-11/71L(+)	8/58-5/59HD(+) 11/71-1/72BK(+)	5/59-4/71D	4/71-7/71PR(+)	7/71-10/71BK(+)
RLH 54	11/52-8/58HD	8/58-2/59AE(+)	2/59-5/59FY(+)	5/59-4/71D	4/71-3/72PR(+)
RLH 55	11/52-2/56HD	3/56-10/64RD	11/64-10/70D	10/70-4/71D(+)	4/71-9/72PR(+)

RLH 56	11/52-8/58HD 9/68-12/68 Works(+)	8/58-2/59AE(+)	2/59-5/59FY(+)	5/59-7/68D	7/68-9/68D(+)
RLH 57	12/52-8/58HD 9/60-11/64D 8/69-4/71D	8/58-2/59AE(+) 1/65-3/66HD 4/71-8/71PR(+)	2/59-5/59FY(+) 3/66D 8/71-10/71BW(+)	5/59-2/60D 3/66-6/69HD	4/60-9/60RG 6/69-8/69SE(+)
RLH 58	12/52-8/58HD	8/58-2/59AE(+)	2/59-5/59FY(+)	5/59-4/71D	4/71-9/72PR(+)
RLH 59	12/52-6/56AL 4/61-8/61HD	8/56-8/58HD 8/61-4/65RD	8/58-2/59AE(+) 6/65-6/69HD	2/59-5/59FY(+) 6/69-9/69SE(+)	5/59-4/61D
RLH 60	12/52-6/56HD	8/56-10/60RD	12/60-6/69HD	6/69-12/69SE(+)	
RLH 61	12/52-7/56HD 1/64-8/65D	8/56-8/58AL 10/65-3/66HD	8/58-3/63HD 3/66-4/71D	3/63-11/63AE(+) 4/71-5/71PR(+)	11/63-1/64SE(+)
RLH 62	12/52-7/56HD	8/56AL	8/58-6/69HD	6/69-8/69SE(+)	8/69-10/69W(+)
RLH 63	12/52-7/56HD 6/69-7/69SE(+)	9/56-8/58AL	8/58-6/61D	6/61-9/65HD	11/65-6/69HD
RLH 64	12/52-7/56HD	9/56-8/58AL	8/58-9/65HD	11/65-4/71D	4/71-9/72PR(+)
RLH 65	12/52-8/58HD 7/69-8/69D	8/58-2/59AE(+) 8/69-11/69D(+)	2/59-5/59FY(+) 11/69-11/70CT(+)	5/59-8/64D 12/70-7/71L(+)	10/64-7/69RD
RLH 66	12/52-8/56HD	9/56-8/58AL	8/58-5/65HD	7/65-4/71D	4/71-9/72PR(+)
RLH 67	12/52-5/55HD 4/71-10/72PR(+)	5/55-8/56RD	10/56-8/58AL	8/58-10/65HD	12/65-4/71D
RLH 68	12/52-8/58AL 9/70-4/71PR(+)	8/58-5/59HD 4/71-5/71BK(+)	5/59-11/65D	1/66-6/69HD	6/69-9/70RD
RLH 69	12/52-8/58AL 4/71-7/71PR(+)	8/58-7/61HD 7/71-11/71BK(+)	7/61-1/65D 11/71-12/71L(+)	2/65-9/70RD 12/71-1/72BK(+)	9/70-4/71D
RLH 70	12/52-10/56AL 7/69-11/69D(+)	11/56-12/64HD	12/64-3/65RD	4/65-7/68HD	7/68-7/69D
RLH 71	12/52-8/58AL 4/71-7/71PR(+)	8/58-3/66HD 7/71-1/72L(+)	3/66-9/70RD	9/70-2/71PR(+)	2/71-4/71D
RLH 72	12/52-9/56AL	10/56-8/61RD	10/61-2/71D	2/71-4/71D(+)	4/71-9/72PR(+)
RLH 73	12/52-9/56AL 10/70-11/70U(+)	11/56-11/60HD	1/61-9/61D	9/61-9/70RD	9/70-10/70PR(+)
RLH 74	12/52-10/56AL	11/56-6/69HD	6/69-12/69SE(+)		
RLH 75	12/52-10/56AL	12/56-1/66HD	1/66D	1/66-7/66D(+)	
RLH 76	12/52-2/55AL 4/66-6/66D(+)	2/55-10/56RD	12/56-8/58AL	8/58-3/62RD	5/62-4/66D

GARAGE CODES

Country Area (Green)				Central Area (Red)			
DS	Dorking	RG	Reigate	AE	Hendon	L	Loughton
EG	East Grinstead	SV	Stevenage	AL	Merton	PR	Poplar
GD	Godstone	WR	Windsor	BK	Barking	RD	Hornchurch
GF	Guildford	WY	Addlestone	BW	Bow	SE	Stonebridge
GR	Garston			CT	Clapton	U	Upton Park
GY	Grays			D	Dalston	W	Cricklewood
MA	Amersham			FY	Finchley		
RE	Romford			HD	Harrow Weald		

(+) Indicates the vehicle was stored unlicenced.

Vehicles were quite often delicenced before entering works for overhaul, thence returning after overhaul and relicenced on the 1st of the following month for tax purposes.
e.g. RLH 1 left MA for overhaul during September 1956 re-entering service on 1st November at Harrow Weald.

TO PASTURES NEW – 1971 ONWARDS
INCLUDING FULL DETAILS OF DISPOSALS

Completing service with either London Transport or London Country was by no means the end of the working life of most RLHs. The majority of the vehicles remaining have spent more years in private ownership than their time spent working on the London suburban and country routes.

Out of the seventy-six vehicles only six went directly to the Yorkshire scrapyard of Wombwell Diesels. A further nine were scrapped during the seventies and a further thirty-five have been or are awaiting the scrap man. This leaves twenty-six RLHs thought to be in existence.

The number of preserved RLHs is steadily growing and since RLH 23 was purchased for preservation in 1967 a further three are now preserved in this country with at least one further example in the USA. There are also others which and may well be preserved in future years.

Vehicles which were exported for a variety of reasons may well remain with their original owners and a small number of these have been confirmed as still in existence. RLH 61 was withdrawn from its touring work in Canada in the autumn of 1983 and it is hoped that the bus has survived with new owners.

RLH DISPOSALS

RLH 1   12/64 Gliksten & Sons (Hardwoods) Ltd, Carpenters Road, London E15.
              12/69 O'Conner, Ilford and subsequently for scrap.

RLH 2   2/65 Passenger Vehicle Sales (London) Ltd, 168/170 Upminster Road, Upminster, Essex.
              2/65 S. Ledgard, Armley, Leeds, Yorkshire.
              10/67 West Yorkshire Road Car Company Ltd. (Not operated but stored pending sale.)
              4/68 P.V.S. (Dealers), Canvey Island, Essex.
              4/68 Nancy Taylor Business Institute, Plainfield, New Jersey, USA.
      by 7/69 Jimmy Byrne, Sea Girt Inn, State Highway 71, Sea Girt, New Jersey, USA.
      by 10/87 Derelict on site of Sea Girt Inn, New Jersey, USA.

RLH 3   2/65 Passenger Vehicle Sales (London) Ltd, 168/170 Upminster Road, Upminster, Essex.
              2/65 Super Coaches, Upminster, Essex.
              1/68 Newport National Bank, Newport Beach, California, USA. (Licence No ZXK 939).
              2/70 Far West Services Inc, Santa Ana, California, USA.
              6/70 Harbor Island Hosts Inc, San Diego, California, USA.
              1/72 Walnut Properties, Beverley Hills, California, USA.
      by 2/73 Aztec Bus Lines, San Diego, California, USA.
              9/73 Seen for sale at a used car lot in Encino, California and not traced further.
     by 1990 Believed to be in the Santa Rosa area of California.

RLH 4   12/64 Passenger Vehicle Sales (London) Ltd, 168/170 Upminster Road, Upminster, Essex.
              12/64 S. Ledgard, Armley, Leeds, Yorkshire.
              10/67 West Yorkshire Road Car Company Ltd. (Not operated but stored pending sale.)
              4/68 P.V.S. (Dealers), Canvey Island, Essex.
              8/68 Ye Olde Kansas City Touring Association, Kansas City, USA.
              –/69 Unknown owner in Norman, Oklahoma, USA and used to carry students between an apartment complex and the University campus.

RLH 5   2/67 Seth Coaches Ltd, 41 Lismore Road, Kentish Town, London NW5.
              4/69 R. E. Doyle (Dealers), St Pancras Way, London NW1 (scrapped).

RLH 6   12/64 Passenger Vehicle Sales (London) Ltd, 168/170 Upminster Road, Upminster, Essex.
              1/65 S. Ledgard, Armley, Leeds, Yorkshire.
              10/67 West Yorkshire Road Car Company Ltd. (Not operated but stored pending sale.)
              4/68 P.V.S. (Dealers), Canvey Island, Essex.
              8/68 Ye Olde Kansas City Touring Association, Kansas City, USA.
      by 1/70 Samual A. Montague, Holiday Camps USA, Kamsco City, Missouri, USA.
      by 4/70 Cheshire Inn and Lodge, St Louis, Missouri, USA. (Licence No 464-002) carried fleet number TRL 560 and inscription 'Bus No 2'.
      by 4/91 Seen at St. Charles, Missouri in reasonable condition (Licence No OFX 381). Later seen September 1991 advertising Deckers Restaurant.

RLH 7	10/67	Long Beach Public Transit Corporation, Long Beach, California, USA. (Licence No E 518144). Shipped out on final voyage of RMS *Queen Mary* from Southampton Docks.
	1/75	Pioneer Theatres Inc, Gardena, California, USA and used on a park and ride service to and from the HMB Interlandia Roadium Swop Meet on Redondo Beach Boulevard, Gardena.
by	6/83	In a scrapyard at 4000 Kettner Boulevard, San Diego, California, USA.
c	1987	Duncans Movie Magic (VHS movie rentals and 1 hour photo), Topeka, Kansas – painted red all over.

RLH 8	12/64	Passenger Vehicle Sales (London) Ltd, 168/170 Upminster Road, Upminster, Essex.
	1/65	S. Ledgard, Armley, Leeds, Yorkshire.
	10/67	West Yorkshire Road Car Company Ltd. (Not operated but stored pending sale.)
	4/68	P.V.S. (Dealers) Canvey Island, Essex, repainted red and given fleet number RLH 51.
	6/68	Mariemont Inn, Wooster Pike, Cincinatti, Ohio, USA.
	1969	Boise Cascade Company, Ocean City, Maryland – used as a courtesy bus at Ocean Pines.
	?	Tom Troxall, Coopersburg, Pennsylvania, USA.

RLH 9	7/66	Leyland Motors Ltd, Berkeley Square House, Berkeley Square, London.
	7/66	Exported to USA.
	–	Jim Hellinger, St Petersburgh Beach, Florida, USA.

RLH 10	2/66	Dagenham Motors, Sangley Road, London SE6.
	2/66	Elkes Biscuits, Uttoxeter, Staffordshire for staff transport.
	1/71	Withdrawn and sold locally for scrap.

RLH 11	5/66	Massey Junior College, 181 Peachtree Street, Atlanta, Georgia, USA. Retained London Transport green livery, still owned January 1974.
by	9/78	'Den of Antiquity', State Highway 170, Beaufort, South Carolina and used as a furniture store. Licence No SC6213.

RLH 12	2/66	Dagenham Motors, Sangley Road, London SE6.
	2/66	Elkes Biscuits, Cardiff, Glamorgan, then to Burscough depot near Southport, Lancashire for staff transport.
	10/71	Bradshaw's Motors (Dealer), Lower Penwortham, Preston, Lancashire for scrap.

RLH 13	1/71	Passenger Vehicle Sales (London) Ltd, Silver End, Essex.
	3/71	Trebor-Sharps Ltd, Woodford Green, Essex, for staff transport to and from former Clarnico factory at Stratford.
	11/73	E. H. Brakell, Cheam, Surrey. (Stored at London Bus Preservation Group premises at Cobham, Surrey.)
	12/74	A.S.B. vitzenbureau, Nieuwe Parklaan 97, s'Gravenhage, Holland for use as a promotional bus. Still owned July 1978 when seen in Leiden, Holland.

RLH 14	1/71	Passenger Vehicle Sales (London) Ltd, Silver End, Essex.
	9/71	Transferred to PVS's Lesney contract fleet, painted blue/yellow.
	9/72	Returned to PVS dealing stock ex Lesney contract fleet, repainted red.
	10/72	Sent to Saltzburg, Austria for a 'British week'.
	10/72	Hired to Peinelt Motors, Munich, Germany for film work, returning to PVS February 1973.

RLH 10 whilst on staff transport duties for Elkes biscuits.

RLH 36 in Hawaii, January 1980.

	4/73	Pennsylvania State University, University Park, State College, Pennsylvania, USA – still owned March 1974.
RLH 15	3/65	Passenger Vehicle Sales (London) Ltd, 168/170 Upminster Road, Upminster, Essex.
	3/65	Super Coaches, Upminster, Essex.
	4/67	Passenger Vehicle Sales (London) Ltd, 168/170 Upminster Road, Upminster, Essex.
	5/67	G. L. Woodford, Newport National Bank, Newport Beach, California, USA.
by	3/75	Tropicana Village, San Luis Obispo, California, USA.
	–/77	British Double Decker Tours Inc, Vancouver, British Columbia, Canada for use on sightseeing tours.
	–/79	Marguerite Tours Ltd, Victoria, Vancouver Island, BC, Canada but not operated.
	9/79	Cunningham, Port Townsend, Washington, USA.
	6/80	Thomas Kohr, Wenatchee, Washington, USA.
	6/82	John Dickenson, White Salmon, Washington, USA.
	1/90	Mike Hackett, Milwaukie, Oregon, USA.
	11/90	Jerry Barron, Portland, Oregon, USA. Still owned September 1994.
RLH 16	2/66	Dagenham Motors, Sangley Road, London SE6.
	2/66	Elkes Biscuits, Uttoxeter, Staffordshire for staff transport.
	12/70	'K.C. Commercials' (Dealer), Belgrave Road, Southampton, Hampshire.
RLH 17	9/67	Elkes Biscuits, Uttoxeter, Staffordshire, then to Burscough depot near Southport, Lancashire for staff transport.
	10/71	Bradshaw's Motors (Dealer), Lower Penwortham, Preston, Lancashire for scrap. Remains passed to Barraclough, Carlton, Barnsley, Yorkshire for final breaking.

RLH 22 Royal Coach Motor Hotel, Atlanta – 26 September 1972.

RLH 18	9/67	M & M Charter Bus Lines, 1945 Evans Avenue, San Francisco, USA.
by	8/72	Salt Lake Transportation Company, Salt Lake City, Utah – used on Gray Line sightseeing tours, Licence No 263424. Still owned May 1973.
by	7/75	Ownership to Trolley Square Shopping Centre, Salt Lake City, Utah but still operated by Salt Lake Transportation Company.
by	7/89	Believed owned by company at Salt Lake that hires canoes etc, with continued deterioration, leaving the vehicle fit for scrap only. Derelict state 4/93.

RLH 19	10/66	Massey Junior College, 181 Peachtree Street, Atlanta, Georgia, USA. Operated in London Transport green livery. Still in use May 1974.
by	10/74	Sold, not traced further.

RLH 20	5/68	A. Pommer, 898 Hyde Park Avenue, Hyde Park, USA MA 02136. Noted at Clarkes Trading Post, Woodstock, New Hampshire in the summer of 1981 in poor condition. This bus was purchased for preservation with pre-war RT 82, both being kept at the Clarkes Trading Post in Woodstock, New Hampshire, USA.

RLH 21	1/71	Passenger Vehicle Sales (London) Ltd, Silver End, Essex.
	3/71	Trebor-Sharps Ltd, Woodford Green, Essex, for staff transport to and from the former Clarnico factory at Stratford.
	3/73	Passenger Vehicle Sales (London) Ltd, Silver End, Essex. Transferred to PVS's Lesney contract fleet, painted blue/yellow.
	10/74	London Bus Preservation Group, Cobham, Surrey.
	3/75	Omnibus Promotions Ltd, London EC1 for promotion work, also for work on their Sheraton Heathrow Hotel contract at London Airport. Repainted in red London Transport livery.
	11/75	British Promotions, Norfolk, Virginia, USA.
	–	Buckingham Realty, Los Angeles, California, USA.
by	9/79	Associated Students of the University of California, Davis, California, but never used in service. Cannabalised for mechanical spares.
	10/81	Sold by auction, Yuba City, California, USA. Not traced further.

RLH 22	11/67	R. Bramblett, 415 East Paces, Ferry Road N.E., Atlanta, Georgia, USA.
by	1969	Royal Coach Motor Hotel, Atlanta, Georgia, USA. Painted red and cream – still owned 1974.

RLH 23	9/67	David Pring, Kenton, Middlesex for preservation, Overhauled and licensed for PSV work, trading as Timebus Travel, St Albans, Hertfordshire. Still owned September 1994.

RLH 24	1/71	Passenger Vehicle Sales (London) Ltd, Silver End, Essex.
	3/71	Trebor-Sharps Ltd, Woodford Green, Essex, for staff transport to and from Clarnico factory at Stratford.
	3/73	Passenger Vehicle Sales (London) Ltd, Silver End, Essex.
	5/73	Sold to the then British Leyland agents in Geneva, Switzerland and used by a department store in Zurich.
by	8/84	'Shoppyland', a Hypermarket at Schonbuhl, Near Berne, Switzerland.
	7/86	To unknown Mercedes dealer in Berne.
	8/86	To unknown owner/dealer.
	9/86	Marco Ghidorzi, 'London Bus' Basel, Switzerland. Fully rebuilt, with PSV licence, and used for promotion and touring work (Licence No BS1850). Still owned September 1994.

RLH 2 at Otley, Yorkshire on 7 July 1965 working for Samuel Ledgard.

RLH 54 is seen working a promotional journey for IKEA in Brussels, Belgium in October 1984.

RLH 25	1/71	Passenger Vehicle Sales (London) Ltd, Silver End, Essex.
	3/71	Gene-Electra, Brussels, Belgium for use on promotion work.
	3/73	Omnibus Promotions Ltd, London EC1.
	5/73	British Promotions, Norfolk, Virginia, USA.
	–	American Real Estate Corporation, Beaumont, Texas, USA.
	9/76	Beaumont Convention & Visitors' Bureau, Beaumont, Texas, USA. Still owned March 1983.

RLH 26	1/71	Passenger Vehicle Sales (London) Ltd., Silver End, Essex.
	11/71	London Bus Preservation Group, Cobham, Surrey. Fully prepared and repainted into London Transport red livery for export.
	1/72	Bernice P. Bishop Museum, Honolulu, Hawaii – withdrawn c1983/84
c	1984	John Webber's Kailua Wrecker for scrap and believed to have been broken up.

| **RLH 27** | 9/69 | Massey Junior College, 181 Peachtree Street, Atlanta, Georgia, USA. Retained London Transport green livery. Still owned January 1974. |
| by | 9/78 | 'Den of Antiquity', State Highway 170, Beaufort, South Carolina and used as a furniture store. Licence No SC6212. |

| **RLH 28** | 9/67 | M & M Charter Bus Lines, San Francisco, California, USA and used by associated company, Associated Charter Bus Co, Van Nuys, California, USA. Painted red and cream and carried UK registration KYY 517. |
| | 2/71 | Pioneer Theatres Inc, Gardena, California, USA and used on a park and ride service to and from the HMB Interlandia Roadium Swop Meet on Redondo Beach Boulevard, Gardena. Still owned June 1975. |

RLH 29	8/72	Country Bus Preservation Group, Isleworth, Middlesex (for preservation).
	/87	David Pring, St Albans, Hertfordshire (for continued preservation).
	7/88	B.T.S. Ltd, Borehamwood, Hertfordshire (for PSV work).
	6/90	Marco Ghidorzi, 'London Bus' Basel, Switzerland. To be fully rebuilt and used with other RLHs for promotion and tour work. Still owned September 1994.

RLH 30	10/67	Long Beach Public Transit Corporation, Long Beach, California, USA. (Licence No E 518143.) Shipped out on final voyage of RMS *Queen Mary* from Southampton Docks.
	3/74	Norwalk Lions Club, Norwalk, California, USA.
by	10/80	'Olde London Curiosity Shop', Kirkland, Washington, USA and used as a shop downstairs with storage area upstairs. In London Transport red livery with white roof.

| **RLH 31** | 1/71 | Passenger Vehicle Sales (London) Ltd, Silver End, Essex. |
| | 4/71 | Piccadilly Inc., Mariemont Inn, Wooster Pike, Cincinatti, Ohio, USA. Not traced further. |

RLH 32	1/71	Passenger Vehicle Sales (London) Ltd, Silver End, Essex.
	10/71	Lesney Products contract fleet for staff transport. Painted blue/yellow.
	6/73	Ensign Bus Company, Hornchurch, Essex. Continued to work Lesney contracts.
	10/74	London Bus Preservation Group, Cobham, Surrey.
	10/75	G. Harrington, Ham, Richmond, Surrey for conversion to caravan. Conversion partly completed together with red repaint.
	8/76	London Bus Preservation Group, Cobham, Surrey. Stored at Eastbourne, Sussex.
	11/76	P. Gascoine and colleagues from Modelstone Bus Club for preservation. Restored to original condition of London Transport green livery and now garaged at the St Helen's Museum of Transport. Still owned September 1994.

RLH 33   1/71 Passenger Vehicle Sales (London) Ltd, Silver End, Essex.
        6/71 Blue Line Coaches Ltd, Upminster, Essex.
        9/71 Passenger Vehicle Sales (London) Ltd, Silver End, Essex.
    11/71 London Bus Preservation Group, Cobham, Surrey. Fully prepared and repainted into London Transport red livery for export.
        1/72 Bernice P. Bishop Museum, Honolulu, Hawaii. Withdrawn c1983/84.
    c 1984 John Webber's Kailua Wrecker for scrap and believed to have been broken up.

RLH 34   1/71 Passenger Vehicle Sales (London) Ltd, Silver End, Essex.
        4/71 Southern California First National Bank, Costa Mesa, California, USA. Seen November 1974 on display as 'Antiques of the World' – but was for sale.
         – William R. Hamilton, Newport Beach, California, USA.

RLH 35   12/70 16th Reigate Scout Group. (Reigate Grammar School.)
        1/86 David Pring, St Albans, Hertfordshire and Richard Proctor, Chertsey, Surrey.
        3/87 Marco Ghidorzi, 'London Bus' Basel, Switzerland. Complete February 1992.

RLH 36   1/71 Passenger Vehicle Sales (London) Ltd, Silver End, Essex.
        6/71 Blue Line Coaches Ltd, Upminster, Essex.
    11/71 London Bus Preservation Group, Cobham, Surrey. Fully prepared and re-painted into London Transport red livery for export.
        1/72 Bernice P. Bishop Museum, Honolulu, Hawaii. Withdrawn c.1983/84.
    c 1984 John Webber's Kailua Wrecker for scrap and believed to have been broken up.

RLH 37   9/65 Whippet Coaches, Hilton, Hunts.
        6/69 Stripped for spares and remains broken by C. E. Street & Sons (Breakers), Hilton, Hunts.

RLH 38   9/65 Whippet Coaches, Hilton, Hunts.
        5/68 F. Cowley (Dealers), Dunchurch, Warwickshire.
        7/68 P.V.S. (Dealers), Canvey Island, Essex.
        8/68 Ye Olde Kansas City Touring Association, Kansas City, USA.
         – Samual A. Montague, Shawnee Mission, Kansas, USA.
    11/73 British Promotions, Norfolk, Virginia, USA.
         – Unknown owner in Wichita, Kansas, USA.
        3/88 Bus for sale in Wichita following the death of its' owner. Possibly purchased by Grace Baptist Church, Wichita.

RLH 39   1/65 Associated Chartered Bus Company, 14649 Lanark Street, Van Nuys, Nr Burbank, California, USA.
         – Sea World, Mission Bay, San Diego, California, USA.
     1971 Picadilly Square, Fresno, California, USA.

RLH 40   8/65 Richard D. Lewis, Mobile Language Laboratories, London W11. Not traced further.

RLH 41   5/65 Passenger Vehicle Sales (London) Ltd, Silver End, Essex.
        5/65 Super Coaches, Upminster, Essex.
        4/67 Passenger Vehicle Sales (London) Ltd, 168/170 Upminster Road, Upminster, Essex.
        5/67 Mariemont Inn, Wooster Pike, Cincinatti, Ohio, USA.
        6/70 London Bus Company, Shaker Heights, Cleveland, Ohio, USA. Sold a few years later.
    by 2/85 Firestone Tyre Depot, Kettering, Ohio, USA.

	2/91	Sold to unknown US Airforce Captain, possibly for conversion into mobile restaurant. Bus traced December 1991 at Wright-Patterson Air Force Base, Fairborn, Ohio, in as acquired condition.
RLH 42	3/65	Harris Lebus Ltd, Tottenham, London N17 (used as a mobile furniture showroom).
	6/68	Nathan, London W10 (mobile boutique).
	12/68	Sold to unknown owner. Parked initially at premises of A. Weston and Sons, Plough Lane, London SW17. Not traced further.

The two views below show RLH 36 working in Hawaii in January 1980.

RLH 43	9/65	Harris Lebus Ltd, Tottenham, London N17.
	12/68	P.V.S. (Dealers), Canvey Island, Essex.
	3/69	P.V.S. (Holdings), for promotional work in Belgium. Returned to P.V.S. Holdings during 1970.
	/71	British Promotions, Boston, Massachusetts, USA.
	9/71	Denver Burglar Alarms (Stu Jackson Enterprises), Golden, Denver, Colorado, USA. Sold – not traced further.

RLH 44		Remained with London County following conversion to Mobile uniform stores vehicle during the years 1970-1980 (re-numbered 581J).
	1/83	D. J. Tippetts, Swindon, Wiltshire for preservation.
	12/90	David Pring, St Albans, Hertfordshire for continued preservation. Still owned September 1994.

RLH 45	1/71	Passenger Vehicle Sales (London) Ltd, Silver End, Essex.
	1/71	City Coachlines, Upminster, Essex.
	6/71	Blue Line Coaches Ltd, Upminster, Essex.
	6/71	Passenger Vehicle Sales (London) Ltd, Silver End, Essex.
	8/71	Operated by P.V.S. Contracts on behalf of Lesney Products, Hackney, London, E9.
	11/72	Museum of Transport & Technology, Western Springs, Auckland, New Zealand. (Licence No EJ3835)
	by 1989	Sold to unknown owner. Believed to be in the Tauranga area of New Zealand.
	by 4/94	Murdock, Auckland, New Zealand.

RLH 46	1/71	Passenger Vehicle Sales (London) Ltd, Silver End, Essex.
	1/71	City Coachlines, Upminster, Essex.
	6/71	Blue Line Coaches Ltd, Upminster, Essex.
	6/73	Omnibus Promotions Ltd, London EC1.
	8/73	British Promotions, Norfolk, Virginia, USA.
	8/73	Tropicana Village, San Luis Obispo, California, USA. Still owned 1975.
	1977	British Double Decker Tours Inc, Vancouver, British Columbia, Canada. Not used and stored in yard of Marguerite Tours Ltd, Victoria, BC.
	by 9/79	Sold.
	by 4/80	Double Decker Family Restaurants of Canada Ltd. Noted on static display outside the Double Decker Hamburger Restaurant at Langley, BC. Later seen February 1982 at Cloverdale, BC, Canada. Not traced further.

RLH 47	1/71	Passenger Vehicle Sales (London) Ltd, Silver End, Essex.
	11/71	London Bus Preservation Group, Cobham, Surrey. Fully prepared and repainted into London Transport red livery for export.
	1/72	Bernice P. Bishop Museum, Honolulu, Hawaii.
	11/82	Withdrawn when termite-infested 'Norfolk Pine' tree collapsed through the roof!
	c 1984	Remains to John Webber's Kailua Auto Wrecker for scrap and believed to have been broken up.

RLH 48	9/65	Whippet Coaches, Hilton, Hunts.
	7/74	London Bus Preservation Group, Cobham, Surrey. Repainted into a yellow all-over advertising livery for the London Broadcasting Company and used on promotional work.
	3/75	James Walker & Sons Ltd. Sent to Belgium agent to promote 'Johnnie Walker Red Label' whisky. Bus was based at Zellick near Brussels in a red livery.
	12/83	London Bus Preservation Group, Cobham, Surrey in dealer capacity.
	5/84	Richard Proctor, Chertsey, Surrey for preservation. Later restored to London Transport green livery. Still owned September 1994.

RLH 49   5/72   Gedol Italaxin, Firenza, Italia. (Used as a mobile demonstration vehicle.)

RLH 50   1/71   Passenger Vehicle Sales (London) Ltd, Silver End, Essex.
              6/71   Blue Line Coaches Ltd, Upminster, Essex.
              6/71   Passenger Vehicle Sales (London) Ltd, Silver End, Essex.
              9/71   Bass-Charrington International Ltd. Presented by Waikato Breweries Ltd to the Museum of Transport & Technology at Western Springs, Auckland, New Zealand. Licence No FV3835.
              4/94   Remains passed to Murdock, Auckland, New Zealand.

RLH 51   3/65   Office Cleaning Services Ltd, Rufford Street, London N1. (Working in Bristol area from April 1965.)
             12/66   ransferred to Longford, Middlesex depot for mainly contracts in and around London (Heathrow) Airport.
              9/68   P.V.S. (Dealers), Canvey Island, Essex.
              9/68   Poole Lane Autos, Highwood, Essex for scrap.

RLH 52   4/71   Inn on the Quay, Quay Corporation, Vancover, Washington, USA. Still owned in 1975 but in poor condition.
        by   9/91   Believed to be owned by Jerry Barron, Portland, Oregon, USA for restoration.

RLH 53   1/72   I. Perch, Hill Country Wagons to Wings Relic Collection, Morgan Hill, California, USA.
             11/93   Sold by auction when the Wagons to Wings Relic Collection, part of Hill Country was closed down. Thought to have been purchased by a Californian Winery.

RLH 54   3/72   Promorama SA, Brussels, Belgium.
        by   8/72   In use with a children's touring amusement group, acting as a restroom and mobile stores, painted white with red roof and lower body skirt panels and advertising soft drinks and crisps. Licence No K413B. Seen in Belgium at St Idelsbald, August 1972 and at Bredene August 1976. Still in use August 1980 (but now repainted red with white band) seen at De Panne.

The two RLHs alongside an ex-Sydney Leyland ready for service at the Museum of Transport & Technology, Western Springs, Auckland, New Zealand – both withdrawn by 1989.

by 10/84 Promobus PVBA, Waterloo, Belgium. Has been rebuilt with a new raisable roof for use when static and fitted with folding doors to the rear platform. Red all over with Licence No ANC 013. Still owned April 1985.

RLH 55 9/72 Wombwell Diesel Company (Dealer), Wombwell, Yorkshire (for scrap).

RLH 56 12/68 P.V.S. (Dealers), Canvey Island, Essex. (Used for spares only.)
11/70 Remains to local breakers.

RLH 57 11/71 Bruce Mulhearn Inc, Realtor, Bellflower, California, USA. Still owned June 1975. Not traced further.

RLH 58 9/72 Wombwell Diesel Company (Dealer), Wombwell, Yorkshire (for scrap).

RLH 59 9/69 Massey Junior College, 181 Peachtree Street, Atlanta, Georgia, USA. Severely damaged in accident and subsequently used for spares, also as a seat store; still owned May 1974.

RLH 60 12/69 Long Beach Public Transit Corporation, Long Beach, California, USA.
2/75 British Promotions, Fountain Valley, California, USA (Dealer).
by 7/75 London Line Realty, El Toro, California, USA.
1978 Sold.
by 9/80 Blue Carpet Mobile Homes, Stanton, California. Painted red with white roof and black waist band.
by 4/85 Kobeys Swapmeet at the Sports Arena, San Diego, California, USA. Still owned August 1989.

RLH 61 4/71 Quo Vardis Club, Bloor Street West, Toronto, Ontario, Canada.
9/73 D. W. Johnson, Toronto, Ontario, Canada.
by 9/74 Travelways Tours Ltd, Thornhill, Ontario – used on tours in Ottawa in 1974 and Kingston, Ontario during 1975 season. Returned to Thornhill by March 1976 and during the following years the bus operated in Ottawa and Kingston for various Travelways companies, including Capitol Coach Lines and Travelways Maple Leaf Ltd. Withdrawn after 1983 season.
9/84 B. Taylor, 'Strawberry Fields', Picton, Ontario, Canada.
10/86 Toronto Double Deck Services, Toronto, Ontario – subsequently seen parked on premises of Fuhrman Auto Centre, Front Street, Toronto, labelled 'FOR SALE'.
-/87 Believed to have been sold at auction.
-/90 Believed to be located in Oshawa, Ontario, Canada.

RLH 62 12/69 Columbus Transit Co, Columbus, Ohio, USA.

RLH 63 7/69 National Diversified Corporation, 2011 Riverside Drive, Columbo, Ohio, USA, for Arthur Treacher's Fish & Chips Inc of the same address.
by 8/73 C. F. Egburt, Route 3, Lucasville, Ohio, USA.
by 8/77 Playpenn, Diamond Beach, New Jersey, USA.

RLH 64 9/72 Wombwell Diesel Company (Dealer), Wombwell, Yorkshire (for scrap).

RLH 65 7/71 Massey Junior College, 181 Peachtree Street, Atlanta, Georgia, USA. Still in use May 1974. Not traced further.

RLH 66 9/72 Wombwell Diesel Company (Dealer), Wombwell, Yorkshire (for scrap).

RLH 67 9/72 Wombwell Diesel Company (Dealer), Wombwell, Yorkshire (for scrap).

Super Coaches of Upminster operated a number of RLHs in their blue and light cream livery. RLH 41 is shown above in this livery alongside RT 1431 (also now preserved) at Brighton following the 1966 HCVC Run.

RLH 73 was sold in November 1970 for conversion to a promotional vehicle in West Germany. The photograph shows the RLH at the University Campus at Saarbrücken, West Germany, in July 1975 following conversion with the lower deck now designated a 'tasting room'.

RLH 6 at Cheshire Lodge, St Louis, Missouri, USA on 29 September 1972.

Several RLHs reached Canada and RLH 61, which was regularly used for touring during the summer months, is seen at Kingston where the 1000 Islands Tours commence. RLH 61 was withdrawn after the 1983 season and its fate is now unsure.

RLH 68	6/71	City of Hampton, Department of Commerce, Hampton, Virginia, USA. Used on narrated tours of Langley Air Force base and NASA's Langley research center. Still owned late 1974.
	by 12/76	Seen at Busch Gardens, 'The Old Country' Theme Park, Route 60, Williamsburgh, Virginia, USA.
RLH 69	1/72	I. Perch, Hill Country Wagons to Wings Relic Collection, Morgan Hill, California, USA.
	11/93	Sold by auction when the Wagons to Wings Relic Collection, part of Hill Country was closed down. Thought to have been purchased by a Californian Winery.
RLH 70	11/69	E. Ansell, Garden Frere, Long Beach, California, USA.
	by 10/80	Static exhibit outside 'The Jolly Knight' Restaurant and Pub, Garden Grove, California – painted red with white roof.
	by 1/92	Rose & Crown Pub, South State College Boulevard, Anaheim, California, USA.
RLH 71	1/72	I. Perch, Hill Country Wagons to Wings Relic Collection, Morgan Hill, California, USA.
	11/93	Sold by auction when the Wagons to Wings Relic Collection, part of Hill Country was closed down. Thought to have been purchased by a Californian Winery.
RLH 72	9/72	Wombwell Diesel Company (Dealer), Wombwell, Yorkshire (for scrap).
RLH 73	11/70	Brauere Felschlosochen, Oggersheim, Germany.
	7/75	Seen at Saarbrücken, University Campus, following conversion for Walsheim, with lower deck designated a 'tasting room'. Not traced further.
RLH 74	12/69	Massey Junior College, 181 Peachtree Street, Atlanta, Georgia, USA.
RLH 75	7/66	Leyland Motors Ltd, Berkeley Square House, Berkeley Square, London. Exported to USA.
	8/66	Seen at a brewery in Natick, Massachusetts. Seen in Boston September 1966 promoting Carlings Beer.
	by 7/84	Derelict with Chicago Motor Coach Company, Chicago, Illinois, still in London Transport red livery; had been used for spares. Remains disposed of.
RLH 76	6/66	Dagenham Motors, 7-12 Sangley Road, London SE6.
	6/66	Elkes Biscuits, Uttoxeter, Staffordshire for staff transport.
	8/67	Transferred to Burscough Depot, near Southport for staff transport.
	4/73	Bloor (Scrap Dealer), Spath, Nr Uttoxeter, Staffordshire. Still intact September 1994 although in poor condition.

REBUILT RLHs

RLH 24, having reached the age of thirty-four years, was purchased by a new owner in Basel, Switzerland. Once purchased the owner decided RLH 24 was a worthy candidate for a complete rebuild and during a three year period the original body was lifted off the chassis, completely rebuilt and enchanced with many modern luxury items. Although not 'original' RLH 24 is a very fine example of the remaining vehicles within the class.

——— · ———

Following the completion of RLH 24, a further bus was purchased, RLH 29, which is currently in the process of a similar rebuild. RLH 29 once completed will join RLH 24 on sightseeing and tour work through the streets of Basel, Switzerland.

The photograph shows RLH 24 with the exterior complete and before receiving its Swiss registration. Basel in Switzerland is the location of this Christmas 1989 view.

Body is completely stripped down to framework.

All that remains of the original body before rebuilding commences.

Body removed with framework receiving steam-clean.

The complete rebuilding of one RLH is probably the largest task undertaken to preserve an example of this class. RLH24 has received this treatment with the rebuilding of a second RLH, this time RLH 29 is now well underway, and the photographs show work in progress during 1990 and 1991.

Rebuilding commenced.

A view of RLH 24 showing rebuilding work in progress at the Basel workshops, Switzerland in May 1988.

The rebuild of RLH 24 was completed in the spring of 1990 following three years of much hard work. During the rebuild RLH received improved heating, an emergency exit door on the offside (which is very cleverly built into one complete bay), intercom systems which link the driver's cab and platform with both decks, and in addition full carpeting.

RLH 24 is now available for hire from London-Bus in Basel where, whilst on tour, owner 'Marco' will put the vehicle in a class of its own – particularly with a tape playing the 'Sounds of London's Big Ben' chiming away whilst RLH 24 follows the trams in Basel!!

(opposite)

RLH 24 completely rebuilt – gleams in readiness for transporting VIPs to the wedding. Basle, Switzerland – Summer 1990.

Another view showing the offside centre emergency exit which is required on PSVs licensed in Switzerland.

These two views show RLH 29 receiving attention firstly at Richmond, Surrey and secondly at the Cobham Bus Museum.

RLH 29 (opposite) was preserved by the Country Bus Preservation Group between July 1972 and August 1986, receiving a body and engine overhaul at the Cobham Bus Museum. During 1990, RLH 29 was also purchased by London-Bus of Basel, Switzerland and driven from Cobham, Surrey to Basel by the new owner.

RLH 35 was also purchased by London-Bus in Basel and is providing valuable assistance whilst the rebuilding of RLHs 24 and 29 takes place. The view below shows the bus in the Basel workshops in May 1988.

REMAINING BRITISH EXAMPLES

Preserved RLH 32 leads RLH 23 and 29 across Staines Bridge on 7 September 1980.

RLH 32 resides in the North West of England and is shown departing Croxteth Park, Liverpool shortly after being repainted.

The first RLH to be preserved, RLH 23 at Brighton, Sussex on 4 May 1969.

Since 1969 RLH 23 has received two further overhauls, and is now returned to PSV operation once again with the same owner, operating as Timebus Travel (Tel: 0727 867941).

RLH 44 which is now preserved in its converted condition as a Mobile Uniform Store.

(opposite top)

RLH 48, initially preserved in red livery, visited Montreux, Switzerland in connection with a promotion for WEA Records. This view shows RLH 48 at Montreux Trolleybus Depot on 4 October 1986.

(opposite lower)

RLH 48 returned to Country Area Livery departs Addlestone Garage in April 1989 during the London Country Open Day.

RLH 76 remains in the scrapyard just outside Uttoxeter where it has now resided unmoved for twenty years. This view was taken in February 1992.

The model 'RLH' built from Anbrico white metal 4mm scale kit.

SPECIAL EVENTS

To mark the passing of the Country Area RLH, ten years to the day a special anniversary tour was organised using RLH 32. The tour covered routes operated by Addlestone Garage with several of the former RLH drivers returning to the wheel during the evening.

10 Year Anniversary Tour

using preserved

MXX 232   (RLH 32)

Thursday, 31st July, 1980

You are invited to join a Special Tour to remember the 'Country RLH' which will depart Addlestone London Country Bus Garage at 1800 returning 21.40.

Organised by
Modelstone Bus Club

MS 1250

1	CB I	26
2		25
3		24
4		23
5	LONDON TRANSPORT COUNTRY BUSES Available from section indicated by punch hole and must be shown on demand. NOT TRANSFERABLE	22
6		21
7		20
8		19
9		18
10		17
11		16
12		15
13		14

Invited guests on RLH 32.

A similar Anniversary Tour marked the passing of RLHs in Central area service. Held ten years after the withdrawal of the 178, RLHs 23 and 29 toured that Dalston route and its short working on 19 April 1981. Some deviations were already necessary because of road alterations.

To The Church On Time

Get Me To The Church On Time!
RLH 32 was used to convey guests from church to the reception at Southport in 1979.

To The Isle of Man

Up, Up and Away – RLH 32 is loaded on to a cargo boat at Heysham for shipment to the Isle of Man where it was to be used on a special holiday tour in 1979.

Arriving at Douglas, Isle of Man.

'Vintage Transport Scene in the Isle of Man.' Here RLH 32 is seen alongside one of the Douglas horse trams.

In 1974 RLH 48 was purchased by the London Bus Preservation Group and was then immediately leased to LBC Radio for promotional work in the London area. For this RLH 48 was repainted in a bright yellow livery, remaining so until March 1975. It is seen here at Uxbridge.

(overleaf)
One of the final Time Tables printed by London Transport in traditional style for an 'RLH' operated route. Here it is for Service 178 produced to inform passengers of the alterations introduced on 4 January 1969.

Bus
178 *to* CLAPTON POND

via Carpenters Road and Hackney Wick

Mondays to Fridays

Stratford *Maryland Station*	0641	0657	0711	0724	0733	0746	0755	0808	0817		0821	0830	0838		0842		0846	0850	0854	0901
Stratford Broadway	0644	0700	0714	0727	0736	0749	0758	0811	0820		0824	0833	0841		0845		0849	0853	0857	0904
Hackney Wick *Eastway*	0654	0710	0725	0738	0747	0800	0809	0822	0831		0835	0844	0852		0856		0900	0904	0908	0915
Homerton Road *Kingsmead Way*	0658	0714	0728	0741	0750	0803	0812	0825	0834		0838	0847	0855		0859		0903	0907	0911	0918
Clapton Pond	0706	0722	0736	0749	0758	0811	0820	0833	0842	†	0844	0855	0903	†	0905	†	0909	0915	†0917	0926 †

						Then				Then								
Stratford *Maryland Station*	0914	0921	0928	0938	0950	every	1226	1237	every	1427	1438	1450	1502	1514		1526
Stratford Broadway	0917	0924	0931	0941	0953	12	1229	1240	10	1430	1441	1453	1505	1517	..	1529
Hackney Wick *Eastway*	0928	0935	0942	0952	1004	minutes	1240	1251	minutes	1441	1452	1504	1516	1528	1535	1540
Homerton Road *Kingsmead Way*	0931	0938	0945	0955	1007	until	1243	1254	until	1444	1455	1507	1519	1531	1537	1543
Clapton Pond	0939	†0944	0953	1003	1015		1251	1302		1452	1503	1515	1527	1539	1545	1551

			MH	FO	MH	MH	FO		MH	FO	FO	MH	FO		FO	MH	FO
Stratford *Maryland Station*	1550	....	1602	1613	1617	1621	1625	1633	1634	1644	1655	1656	1704	1705	1712	1716	1718	1720
Stratford Broadway	1553	....	1605	1616	1620	1624	1628	1636	1637	1647	1658	1659	1707	1708	1715	1719	1721	1723
Hackney Wick *Eastway*	1604	1611	1616	1627	1631	1635	1639	1647	1648	1658	1709	1710	1718	1719	1726	1730	1732	1734
Homerton Road *Kingsmead Way*	1607	1613	1619	1630	1634	1638	1642	1650	1651	1701	1712	1713	1721	1722	1729	1733	1735	1737
Clapton Pond	1615	1621	1627	1638	1642	1646	1650	1658	1659	1709	1720	1721	1729	1730	1737 †	1739	1743	1745 †

	MH	FO	FO	MH	FO	MH	FO	FO	MH	MH	FO	MH		MH	FO	MH	MH
Stratford *Maryland Station*	1727	1728	1732	1736	1737	1740	1742	1748	1749	1753	1754	1757	1802	1806	1810	1811	1816
Stratford Broadway	1730	1731	1735	1739	1740	1743	1745	1751	1752	1756	1757	1800	1805	1809	1813	1814	1819
Hackney Wick *Eastway*	1741	1742	1746	1750	1751	1754	1756	1802	1803	1807	1808	1811	1816	1820	1824	1825	1830
Homerton Road *Kingsmead Way*	1744	1745	1749	1753	1754	1757	1759	1805	1806	1810	1811	1814	1819	1823	1827	1828	1833
Clapton Pond	1752	1753	†1755	1801	1802	†1803	1807	1813	1814	1818	†1817	†1820	1827	†1829	1835	1836 †	1839

	MH	FO	MH														
Stratford *Maryland Station*	1821	1826	1828	1836	1849	1903	1918	1933	1948	2010	2035	....	..	..	....	....	....
Stratford Broadway	1824	1829	1831	1839	1852	1906	1921	1936	1951	2013	2038	..	..	..	....	....	....
Hackney Wick *Eastway*	1835	1840	1842	1850	1903	1916	1931	1946	2001	2023	2048	..	..	..	....	....	....
Homerton Road *Kingsmead Way*	1838	1843	1845	1853	1906	1919	1934	1949	2004	2026	2051	..	..	..	....	....	....
Clapton Pond	1846	†1851		1901	1914	1927	1942	1957	2012	2034	2059						

Saturdays

Stratford *Maryland Station*	0641	0658	0715	0728	0741	0755	0810	0825	0840	0855	0910	0925	0940	0955	1015	1036	1057	1117
Stratford Broadway	0644	0701	0718	0731	0744	0758	0813	0828	0843	0858	0913	0928	0943	0958	1018	1039	1100	1120
Hackney Wick *Eastway*	0653	0710	0727	0740	0753	0807	0822	0837	0852	0907	0923	0938	0953	1008	1028	1049	1110	1130
Homerton Road *Kingsmead Way*	0656	0713	0730	0743	0756	0810	0825	0840	0855	0910	0926	0941	0956	1011	1031	1052	1113	1133
Clapton Pond	0704	0721	0738	0751	0804	0818	0833	0848	0903	0918	0934	0949	1004	1019	1039	1100	1121	1141

		Then			Then										
Stratford *Maryland Station*	1155	every	1410	1429	every	1849	1909	1929	1949	2011	2035	....	....	....	....
Stratford Broadway	1158	15	1413	1432	20	1852	1912	1932	1952	2014	2038	...	..	....	....
Hackney Wick *Eastway*	1208	minutes	1423	1442	minutes	1902	1921	1941	2001	2023	2047	...	..	....	....
Homerton Road *Kingsmead Way*	1211	until	1426	1445	until	1905	1924	1944	2004	2026	2050	..	..	....	....
Clapton Pond	1219		1434	1453		1913	1932	1952	†2010	†2032	† 2056				

†—Time at Clapton *Urswick Road.* **MH**—Mondays to Thursdays. **FO**—Fridays only.

ADDITIONAL BUSES : Stratford *Maryland Station* to Hackney Wick *Victoria Hotel* : Monday to Friday 0651, 0715, 0719, 0728, 0737, 0742, 0751, 0759, 0804, 0813, 0826, 0834 ; Monday to Thursday 1629, 1638, 1649, 1700, 1709, 1713, 1722, 1731, 1744 ; Friday only 1617, 1625, 1630, 1639, 1652, 1700, 1708.

NOTE : No service operates on Sundays or Bank Holidays. While every effort will be made to keep to the timetables, London Transport does not undertake that its buses will be operated in accordance with them, or at all. London Transport will not be responsible for any loss, damage or inconvenience caused by reason of any operating failure or in consequence of any inaccuracies in the timetables.

LONDON TRANSPORT, 55 BROADWAY, S.W.1. *Telephone :* 01-222 1234 4.1.69.

1268/4148p/450   8971   Knapp, Drewett & Sons Ltd., London and Kingston upon Thames. 28066R.

s

78 to STRATFORD (Maryland Station)

via Hackney Wick and Carpenters Road

Mondays to Fridays

									MH	FO								
pton Pond	0614	†0625	0638	†0638	0642	†0648	†0652	0654	0703	0704	†0709	0716	†0723	0729	0743	0756	0805	0818
merton Road *Kingsmead Way*	0622	0631	0633	0644	0650	0654	0658	0702	0711	0712	0715	0724	0729	0737	0751	0804	0813	0826
kney Wick *Eastway*	0625	0634	0641	0647	0653	0657	0701	0705	0714	0715	0718	0727	0732	0740	0754	0807	0816	0829
tford Broadway	0635	0644	0651	0657	0703	0707	0712	0716	0725	0726	0729	0738	0743	0751	0805	0818	0827	0840
atford *Maryland Station*	0637	0646	0653	0659	0705	0709	0714	0718	0727	0728	0731	0740	0745	0753	0807	0820	0829	0842

																	MH
pton Pond	0826	0837	0852	0900	0910	Then every 12 minutes until	1158	1208	Then every 10 minutes until	1358	1410	1422	1434	1446	1458	1510	1520
merton Road *Kingsmead Way*	0834	0845	0900	0908	0918		1206	1216		1406	1418	1430	1442	1454	1506	1518	1528
kney Wick *Eastway*	0837	0848	0903	0911	0921		1209	1219		1409	1421	1433	1445	1457	1509	1521	1530
tford Broadway	0848	0859	0914	0922	0932		1220	1230		1420	1432	1444	1456	1508	1520	1532	..
atford *Maryland Station*	0850	0901	0916	0924	0934		1222	1232		1422	1434	1446	1458	1510	1522	1534	..

	FO										MH	FO		MH	FO		MH	FO	MH
pton Pond	†1522	1522	1533	1544	†1550	1552	†1556	†1558	1600	†1607	1609	1610	†1616	†1617	1620	1625	1628	1635
merton Road *Kingsmead Way*	1528	1530	1541	1552	1556	1600	1602	1604	1608	1613	1617	1618	1622	1623	1628	1633	1636	1643
kney Wick *Eastway*	1530	1533	1544	1555	1559	1603	1604	1607	1611	1616	1620	1621	1625	1626	1631	1636	1639	1646
tford Broadway	..	1544	1555	1606	1610	1614	..	1618	1622	1627	1631	1632	1636	1637	1642	1647	1650	1657
atford *Maryland Station*	..	1546	1557	1608	1612	1616	..	1620	1624	1629	1633	1634	1638	1639	1644	1649	1652	1659

	FO	MH	FO		MH	FO	MH			FO	MH	FO	MH	FO	MH	FO			
pton Pond	1636	1643	1644	1652	1656	1704	1705	1714	1726	1727	1733	1736	1742	1747	1750	1759	1807	1820	1835
merton Road *Kingsmead Way*	1644	1651	1652	1700	1704	1712	1713	1722	1734	1735	1741	1744	1750	1755	1758	1807	1815	1828	1843
kney Wick *Eastway*	1647	1654	1655	1703	1707	1715	1716	1725	1737	1738	1744	1747	1753	1858	1801	1810	1818	1831	1846
tford Broadway	1658	1705	1706	1714	1718	1726	1727	1736	1748	1749	1755	1758	1804	1809	1812	1821	1829	1842	1857
atford *Maryland Station*	1700	1707	1708	1716	1720	1728	1729	1738	1750	1751	1757	1800	1806	1811	1814	1823	1831	1844	1859

pton Pond	1851	1906	1921	1943	2007	..	..	..	..	..	..	..	..	..	..	..	..	..
merton Road *Kingsmead Way*	1859	1914	1929	1951	2015	..	..	..	..	..	..	..	..	..	..	..	..	..
kney Wick *Eastway*	1902	1917	1932	1954	2018	..	..	..	..	..	..	..	..	..	..	..	..	..
tford Broadway	1912	1927	1942	2004	2028	..	..	..	..	..	..	..	..	..	..	..	..	..
atford *Maryland Station*	1914	1929	1944	2006	2030	..	..	..	..	..	..	..	..	..	..	..	..	..

Saturdays

pton Pond	0614	0631	0648	0701	0714	0729	0744	0759	0814	0829	0842	0857	0912	0928	0948	1009	1030	1050	1110
merton Road *Kingsmead Way*	0622	0639	0656	0709	0722	0737	0752	0807	0822	0837	0850	0905	0920	0936	0956	1017	1038	1058	1118
kney Wick *Eastway*	0625	0642	0659	0712	0725	0740	0755	0810	0825	0840	0853	0908	0923	0939	0959	1020	1041	1101	1121
tford Broadway	0634	0651	0708	0721	0734	0749	0804	0819	0834	0849	0903	0918	0933	0949	1009	1030	1051	1111	1131
atford *Maryland Station*	0636	0653	0710	0723	0736	0751	0806	0821	0836	0851	0905	0920	0936	0951	1011	1032	1053	1113	1133

pton Pond	1127	Then every 15 minutes until	1342	1401	Then every 20 minutes until	1841	1902	1922	1944	2007	..	..
merton Road *Kingsmead Way*	1135		1350	1409		1849	1910	1930	1952	2015	..	..
kney Wick *Eastway*	1138		1353	1412		1852	1913	1933	1955	2018	..	..
tford Broadway	1148		1403	1422		1902	1922	1942	2004	2027	..	..
atford *Maryland Station*	1150		1405	1424		1904	1924	1944	2006	2029	..	..

MH—Mondays to Thursdays.   **FO—Fridays only.**   **†—Time at Clapton *Urswick Road.***

ADDITIONAL BUSES : Hackney Wick *Victoria Hotel* to Stratford *Maryland Station* : Monday to Friday 0709, 0723, 0736, 0745, 0749, 0758, 0802, 0811, 0820, 0824, 0833, 0844, 0856 ; Monday to Thursday 1642, 1650, 1659, 1712, 1720, 1729, 1734, 1742, 1752, 1803 ; Friday only 1635, 1643, 1651, 1659, 1707, 1711, 1720, 1731.

IDON TRANSPORT, 55 BROADWAY, S.W.I.   *Telephone : 01-222 1234.*   4.1.69.

RLH 20 was sold to Alan Pommer in May 1968 for preservation and this rear view shows the vehicle in a sorry state at The Clarkes Trading Post, Woodstock, New Hampshire, USA awaiting further attention.

Rear Cover:
RLH 29, which is now preserved, seen in 1989 at the North Weald Bus Rally prior to leaving the British Isles in 1990 for Basle in Switzerland. Following a complete rebuild RLH 29 will join RLH 24 on Special Tours and Promotional Work.★ (see pages 60-67).

The story of the 'RLH' is, as yet, not complete for with about twelve of those originally built in 1950 and 1952 remaining in good order today the future for them looks quite promising. Their future will be followed so that the history of the RLH may be recorded and to this end any sightings or information regarding RLHs would be gratefully received by the Author. Please address all communications to

Peter Gascoine
3 Ayrefield Grove
Shevington, Wigan
Lancashire WN6 8DZ